Author:
Alex Woolf studied history at Essex University, England. He is the author of many books for children on science topics, including previous titles in the *Science Of* series on rocks and minerals and natural disasters.

Series creator:
David Salariya was born in Dundee, Scotland. He has illustrated a wide range of books and has created and designed many new series for publishers in the UK and overseas. David established The Salariya Book Company in 1989. He lives in Brighton with his wife, illustrator Shirley Willis, and their son Jonathan.

Artists:
Isobel Lundie, Bryan Beach, Jared Green, Sam Bridges and Shutterstock.

Editor:
Nick Pierce

Published in Great Britain in MMXIX by
Book House, an imprint of
The Salariya Book Company Ltd
25 Marlborough Place, Brighton BN1 1UB
www.salariya.com

PB ISBN: 978-1-912537-60-0

SCRIBO BOOK HOUSE SCRIBBLERS

3 5 7 9 8 6 4 2

A CIP catalogue record for this book is available from the British Library.

Printed and bound in China.

Reprinted in MMXIX.

Visit
www.salariya.com
for our online catalogue and
free fun stuff.

PAPER FROM
SUSTAINABLE
FORESTS

The Science of Buildings

The Sky-Scraping Story of Structures

Written by
Alex Woolf

BOOK HOUSE
a SALARIYA imprint

Contents

Introduction 5

Ancient buildings 6

Medieval buildings 8

A building's life cycle 10

How are buildings designed and planned? 12

Building materials 14

How are buildings constructed? 16

Skyscrapers 18

How do we build in disaster zones? 20

How do we build sustainably? 22

Demolition 24

What is the future of buildings? 26

The future of building materials 28

Glossary 30

Index 32

Introduction

We spend a lot of our lives in buildings, but how many of us really think about how they're built and what they do for us? Buildings provide us with one of our most basic needs – shelter. They protect us from heat, cold, wind and rain. The first buildings were simple homes. As society developed, architects (designers of buildings) needed to create different kinds of structures – from palaces and temples to modern factories, airports and skyscrapers.

In this book we'll explore the science of architecture since ancient times, and examine the life cycle of a building, from design and construction to demolition. We'll look at the challenges faced by today's architects, including how to build in areas prone to natural disasters, and how to build sustainably, so that our structures don't end up damaging the planet.

Greek temple

Ancient Greek temples consisted of a closed rectangular space called a *cella*, surrounded by columns. Architects distorted the lines of temples to counteract the effects of perspective. From below, a long, straight roof would appear to sag, so they'd raise it slightly in the middle to compensate for this effect.

Arches are strong because each stone in the arch pushes hard against the stones on either side. This sideways pressure helps hold the arch together and makes it strong enough to support other columns and arches above it.

Ancient buildings

The earliest houses were built by farmers many thousands of years ago. From around 4000 BC, the Sumerians of Mesopotamia (modern-day Iraq) built the first large-scale buildings, including temples and palaces. Many early buildings were made with sun-dried clay bricks called adobe. The ancient Egyptians constructed enormous pyramids from blocks of stone as tombs for their kings. They may have used the pyramid shape because it is very stable and, unlike other building shapes (such as towers), can be built to enormous scales without risk of collapse. Later, the ancient Greeks and Romans introduced new architectural forms, such as columns and pediments, arches, vaults and domes.

Arch

Column

Pantheon

The Pantheon in Rome was built in 125 CE and has the world's largest unreinforced concrete dome. The dome is stable because the concrete is thick at the base and thin at the top. At the base the Romans used heavy granite as aggregate in the concrete; at the top they mixed it with lightweight volcanic rock instead.

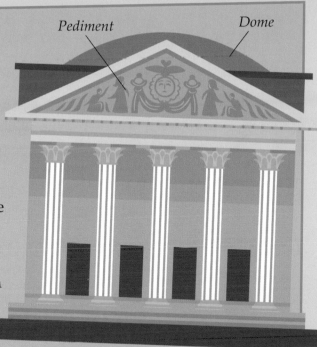

Pediment

Dome

The Romans developed a new building material, concrete, which was as strong as stone, durable and easily formable into different shapes.

Roman Colosseum

The Romans built many new kinds of structures, including public baths, aqueducts, amphitheatres, basilicas and domed temples. One of the most famous of their buildings is the Colosseum in Rome.

Fascinating fact

The Great Pyramid of Giza is the largest of all ancient Egyptian pyramids. It was built for King Khufu in around 2600 BC. It contains over two million stone blocks, each one weighing some 2,267 kilograms (2.5 tons). It originally stood 147 metres (481 feet) high, and its base covers 5 hectares (13 acres).

In 1420, Brunelleschi began constructing the dome of Florence Cathedral out of millions of bricks in a herringbone pattern for extra strength.

Medieval buildings

Building stones

Medieval quarrymen would 'read' the rock face to see the lines where it would fracture. Then they drilled a line of holes and pounded pegs into the holes to make it split. The stones they quarried were hauled to the building site on horse-drawn wagons where stone masons chiselled them into blocks.

D uring the Middle Ages, architects began building castles out of stone, with high walls and round towers to better withstand attacks. With the emergence of Gothic cathedrals, the rounded Roman arch was replaced with the pointed arch, enabling taller and more complex buildings. The cathedrals had pillars that fanned outwards to form ribbed vaults, an innovation that allowed them to span much larger spaces.

Round towers

High walls

Ha! They'll never get in!

8

Treadwheel cranes

These were a medieval innovation that allowed the building of huge castles and cathedrals. A rope is attached to a pulley, which is turned on a spindle by the rotation of a treadwheel turned by someone walking on it. Heavy materials could be lifted into position.

Taj Mahal

The Taj Mahal, the most celebrated example of Mughal architecture in India, was completed in 1648. It was made from brick faced with white marble. A 15 kilometre (9.3 mile) ramp was constructed to transport the material up the plinth on which the building stands. The main dome was built using brick scaffolding.

The chimney first appeared in the 12th century. Before then, dwellings had a central fire pit with a hole in the roof above. Chimneys freed up space and made the air in buildings much less smoky.

Why it works

Gothic cathedrals are tall with thin walls filled with stained glass windows, so how do they stay up? The main weight of the cathedral is supported by the rows of tall internal pillars and by pointed arch vaulting. External flying buttresses protect the buildings from sideways (wind) pressures.

Arch vaulting

Pillars

A building's life cycle

All human-made objects have a 'product life cycle'. The life cycle of a building begins when a property developer decides to purchase some land and construct something on it. This sets in motion a series of processes: raw building materials must be extracted and processed; architects create designs; labourers set to work on the construction; the completed building is occupied and must be maintained, often for decades or even centuries; finally it is demolished, and its materials are recycled or reused in other buildings.

Land

Land for building is purchased and then, if necessary, prepared for use. Marshes are drained and obstacles removed. The land is surveyed, so its shape and natural features are made known to the architect.

Demolition

Buildings eventually become worn out or fall into disuse. They may be restored, repurposed or else demolished.

Parts and materials may be reclaimed by salvage companies for reuse in other buildings. The rest will go to landfill.

Materials

Raw materials, such as stone, clay, iron ore and timber are mined or harvested, then processed to make them suitable for use in construction. For example, clay is fired into bricks, and iron ore is smelted to make iron and steel.

Design

A team of architects design the building. They create it as a model on a computer together with detailed drawings and specifications.

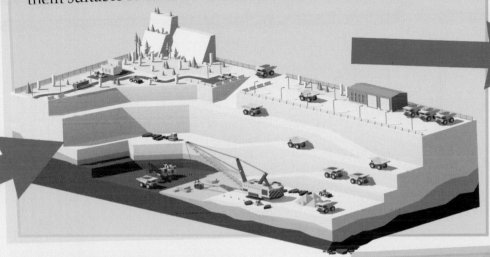

Occupancy and maintenance

During the main stage of a building's life cycle, when it is being used, it must be continually maintained, with its plumbing, heating and electrical systems regularly checked, repaired and, if necessary, replaced.

Construction

A general contractor assembles a team of labourers, together with the necessary materials, machinery and equipment, and the building is constructed.

The team

To help prepare the design, the architect assembles a team of experts. Structural engineers check that walls and floors can support the loads required, and the building will not collapse. Mechanical engineers are experts in electrical, heating, cooling and plumbing systems. Quantity surveyors check the costs of the project to ensure the client gets good value.

CAD is a computer programme that creates 3D geometric shapes much more quickly and accurately than a human hand, and can also render them in different colours and textures.

How are buildings designed and planned?

The process of planning a building begins when a property developer (the client) briefs an architect on what sort of building is required. The architect must design a building that meets the client's needs and budget, provides a secure and healthy environment for its occupants, and complies with local planning laws. Architects also consider the surveyor's report on the size and topography (physical features) of the site; the impact on the local community and environment; and how well the building will fit into its surroundings.

This is my dream house...

But it doesn't fit in here!

Drawings

Architects create technical drawings of the proposed building using computer-aided design (CAD). CAD is any computer program that helps architects create designs, plans and models of buildings. CAD drawings include:

- floor plans: layout of rooms on each floor
- site plan: bird's-eye view of whole site, showing connections to drainage and sewage pipes and power lines
- elevation: external view of building from one side
- cross-section: vertical slice through building
- roof plan: internal structure of roof

3D images

CAD can turn 2D drawings into 3D photorealistic images of the finished building, viewable from any direction, to show to the client and the public. CAD allows architects to delete errors and make changes quickly and easily. But it can encourage architects to add complexity to their designs, and raise expectations of what is practical.

CAD can even generate 3D animations, allowing clients to take a virtual tour of the building, inside and out.

Why it works

Architects often build scale models of the proposed building to visualise it, or help sell it as a design. These can be made from foam, cardboard, paper or wood and built to a variety of scales. Today, architects are using 3D printing techniques to turn their CAD virtual designs into physical scale models.

Couldn't we just print the whole building?

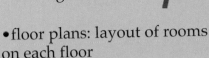

Building materials

Plastic can be moulded or cast into any shape. It is light, hard-wearing and of uniform consistency. It is used for door handles, floor coverings, wall panels, cladding and even big structures such as domes.

Clay

For thousands of years clay has been used to make buildings of adobe, rammed earth and wattle and daub. These days it is used to make bricks, plaster and clay tiles. Clay is strong and extremely durable: brick buildings with tile roofs dating back to Roman times can still be seen today.

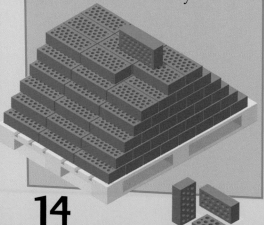

Many different kinds of material are used in the construction of a building, including naturally occurring ones like stone, timber and clay, and synthetic ones like concrete, steel, foam, glass and plastic. When architects decide on whether to use a material, they must think about its cost, durability, availability, environmental impact, suitability for the local climate, how it fits into its surroundings and how it will affect the comfort of the building's users. Stone, for example, retains heat and releases it gradually, keeping homes warm in winter and cool in summer.

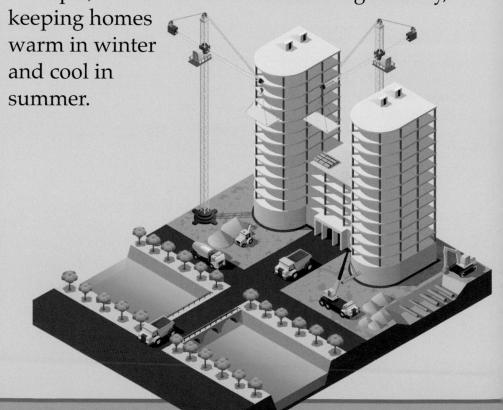

Glass

Glass is brittle, but benefits from being transparent, letting light into buildings. Traditionally, glass windows were small because glass was expensive. Today, it's cheap and can be produced in big sheets. Many public buildings feature glass walls and roofs, giving them a sense of light and space.

Only another 42 floors to go!

Foam is made by trapping gas in liquid plastic or rubber and then solidifying it. Light and easily moulded into different shapes, it is used inside walls to help insulate buildings from cold, heat or noise, or as a fire retardant.

Cement

Cement is a 'binder' – it's used to bind other substances together to form a strong building material, such as mortar, concrete, stucco and grout. Cement sets when mixed with water. The water reacts with the cement, causing it to form interlocking crystals, which gives cement its strength.

Can you believe it?

Straw has been a building material since prehistoric times, and is still used today. It can be compressed to form compact bales that can be used to make walls. It is cheap and a good insulator, though it does catch fire easily and may attract vermin.

Framing

The framework is the building's skeleton, to which the walls, floors, ceilings and roof are attached. The framework is usually made of wood or steel tubes. Vertical wall supports are called studs; horizontal floor and ceiling supports are called joists; and sloping roof supports are called rafters.

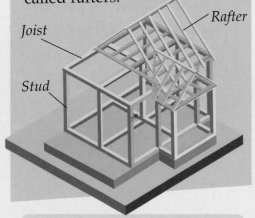

Joist

Rafter

Stud

A building site needs people with many different skills, including bricklayers, carpenters, concrete finishers, ironworkers (for assembling steel frames), plasterers, pipefitters and roofers.

How are buildings constructed?

The first stage of any construction project is preparing the site. Bulldozers clear the site of trees, rocks and other features before digging a pit for the foundation – the base of the building. Trenches are dug to carry cables and pipes to and from the building. The foundation is then laid. This transfers the building's weight to the ground. Structural engineers must ensure the foundation and the soil beneath it are capable of bearing the weight of the building evenly. Generally speaking, the heavier the building or the weaker the underlying soil, the deeper the foundation must be.

Leaning Tower of Pisa, which has a weak foundation.

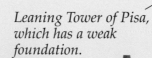

Insides and outsides

The next stage is to construct the building framework, followed by the roof frame, roofing and siding materials, as well as internal structures like pillars and staircases. Windows and doors are usually set in their frames after all the framing is finished to avoid damaging them.

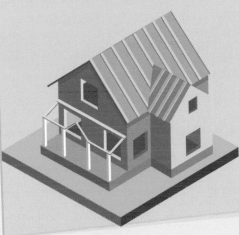

Construction sites can be dangerous. Workers risk falls, electrocution, hearing loss and lung problems from breathing toxic fumes. Workers should wear hard hats and ear protectors.

Finishing touches

The final stage is to make the building fit for habitation: walls are painted, wallpapered or tiled; floors are carpeted; and sockets, light fixtures, radiators, sinks, baths, toilets and kitchen appliances are installed.

Fascinating fact

One of the world's longest ever building construction projects is the Sagrada Família, a Roman Catholic church in Barcelona, Spain. Begun in 1882, the planned completion date is 2026, though it may not be finished until 2040. The architect, Antoni Gaudí, died in 1926, when the church was less than a quarter complete.

Skyscrapers

A few wooden skyscrapers have been built. Brock Commons, an 18-storey, 53-metre (174-feet) student dormitory in Vancouver, Canada, became the world's tallest in 2016.

One of the greatest innovations in architecture in the past 150 years has been the skyscraper. These tall, multi-storey buildings were made possible by the use of steel frameworks to support the buildings' weight. The walls are suspended from the steel frame like curtains. Before this, walls had to support the weight of upper storeys, limiting the potential height of buildings. Another crucial advance was the invention in the 1850s of the safety elevator, which offered people safe, rapid and convenient access to and from the skyscrapers' upper storeys.

Flexible structure

Strong and malleable, steel is useful as a framework for a skyscraper because it lets the building move and bend without collapsing. This flexibility allows skyscrapers to withstand most high winds, earth tremors or aeroplane impacts.

Tubular design

Most skyscrapers built since the 1960s have a structure based on a hollow tube. The perimeter consists of closely spaced columns braced with horizontal beams, forming a sturdy and powerful frame. With no need for internal supporting walls or columns, there is more usable floor space.

This floor will make a nice office.

Burj Khalifa

The Burj Khalifa in Dubai became the tallest building in the world on its completion in 2010. It rises 828 metres (2,716 feet) from the ground and consists of 163 storeys. Unlike many skyscrapers, the Burj Khalifa does not have a steel frame but is supported by a core of reinforced concrete.

Skyscrapers use up a lot of energy! Water has to be pumped to every floor, and elevators are generally used instead of stairs. On the plus side, their large windows reduce the need for lighting.

Can you believe it?

The world's earliest skyscrapers were built in ancient Rome. Some reached ten or more storeys and could be over 25 metres (82 feet) tall. The upper storeys were rented to poor citizens. With no internal water supply or elevators, these were the least comfortable places to live.

Earthquakes

Architects working in quake-prone regions may install dampers – concrete or steel blocks that move in opposition to shock waves by means of springs, fluids or pendulums. They may insert shock-absorbing padded cylinders in the building's base to isolate the rest of the building from its foundations.

How do we build in disaster zones?

Many people live in parts of the world that are prone to natural disasters, including volcanic eruptions, earthquakes, hurricanes, floods and wildfires. Architects designing buildings in these locations face extra challenges to create structures that can resist the worst impacts of such disasters. When time and money are available, architects are able to employ techniques to make buildings safer from future disasters.

Buildings near volcanoes should have strong roofs and shuttered windows to protect against falling ash. Steel frames are more fire resistant than timber.

The perfect house!

Floods

In flood-prone Bangladesh, homes are given sturdy brick-and-concrete foundations and lower walls to prevent them being washed away. Upper walls are cheap, replaceable jute panels fastened to bamboo poles. Houses are surrounded by water-thirsty plants to soak up floodwater.

Hurricanes

Architects in hurricane-hit areas keep roofs fixed to buildings by anchoring them, via the walls, to the foundations. Buildings that are low to the ground, or ones with domed roofs are better able to withstand hurricanes than tall or square buildings. Windows can have plastic panes or shatterproof glass.

In tsunami zones, buildings are often constructed on sturdy support columns. When not threatened by the sea, glass walls can slide down between the pillars to create a downstairs room.

Why it works

How do you make a home resistant to a wildfire to avoid the scene you see below?
• Leave plenty of space between the house and trees.
• Use heat-resistant materials on roofs and walls.
• Install roll-down metal shutters to protect glass doors and windows.
• Protect access points such as vents and cracks in the roof where embers can enter.
• Maintain a sprinkler system.

How do we build sustainably?

Architects can 'design for deconstruction', using recyclable materials and a modular construction that can be easily dismantled at the end of a building's useful life.

Design

To use resources more efficiently, buildings can be fitted with low-flush toilets; lighting controlled by motion detectors; insulated walls and double-glazed windows to minimise heat loss; and windows placed to maximise daylight, reducing the need for electric lighting.

The construction industry has a massive impact on our planet's environment, contributing to air and water pollution, landfill waste and climate change. In recent years architects and builders have been looking at ways of minimising these impacts. Architects are designing buildings that consume energy and water more efficiently during their operational life. Builders are using methods that produce less waste, and sourcing materials locally to reduce the need for transportation. Today, many buildings are deconstructed (taken apart) at the end of their useful life for recycling and reuse.

Deconstruction

Unlike demolition, deconstruction is slow and labour-intensive. Reusable parts must be removed carefully to avoid damaging them. However, it's cost effective because items can be sold. It also reduces the need to extract new materials, which lowers greenhouse gas emissions caused by burning waste in landfills or by the manufacturing of new construction materials.

Construction

Construction sites produce a lot of waste material. Today, governments are encouraging contractors to reduce, reuse and recycle waste rather than send it to a landfill.

Reduce waste by using computer software to estimate quantities of materials accurately and avoid over-ordering.

Reuse materials by collecting off-cuts rather than ordering new.

Recycle waste by sorting different waste materials onsite.

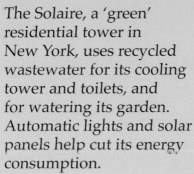

The Solaire, a 'green' residential tower in New York, uses recycled wastewater for its cooling tower and toilets, and for watering its garden. Automatic lights and solar panels help cut its energy consumption.

Try it yourself

Talk to your parents about minimising your home's environmental impact by:
- installing energy-saving lightbulbs
- using low-flow showerheads, taps and toilets
- choosing furnishings that are second-hand, recycled or sustainably produced
- keeping the thermostat low in winter

23

Demolition

The final stage in a building's life cycle is its demolition. This may happen because the building is no longer used or has become unsafe. Before demolition can take place, permissions must be sought from the relevant authorities and the public notified. In the past, buildings were demolished by hand using small tools. Since the early 20th century, big machines have been used, most famously wrecking balls. Larger buildings are demolished using explosives.

Smashing and toppling

Cranes equipped with wrecking balls weighing up to 6,000 kilograms (13,000 pounds) smash into walls, turning buildings to rubble. For taller buildings, high-reach excavators are used, with a demolition arm to which shears or hammers are attached. These slice through steel or shatter concrete.

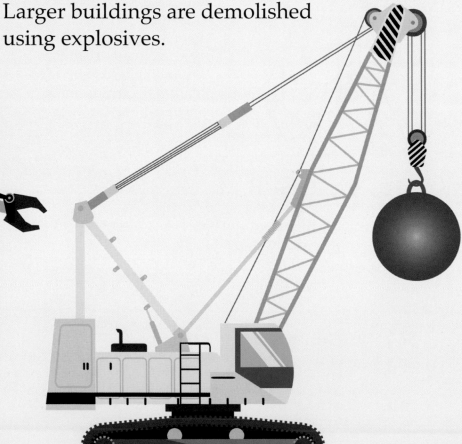

Collapse

Low-rise buildings can be demolished using undermining: hydraulic excavators dig beneath the building's walls, causing it to collapse. Vérinage is a French technique for demolishing high-rise buildings: the supports on the central floors are weakened, causing the top part to collapse. This produces enough weight and momentum to bring down the lower section.

Toppling towers

A tall building can be toppled safely with a series of small, carefully placed explosions to destroy its structural supports, causing it to fall in a controlled way onto its side or vertically.

Explosives, such as nitroglycerin, are used in demolitions. They are placed in holes drilled into columns on the lower floors. The explosives are timed to go off at intervals so the building falls in a certain way. Architectural plans are consulted and 3D models created to see how the building will fall.

Why it works

'Cut-and-take-down' is a safe way of demolishing buildings in built-up areas. Hydraulic jacks support the bottom storey as the support beams are removed. The ceiling is then lowered on the jacks. The process is repeated for each storey. This is less dusty and noisy than other kinds of demolition, and reduces landfill waste.

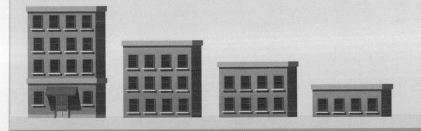

Stage 1   Stage 2   Stage 3   Stage 4   Stage 5

25

What is the future of buildings?

Smart buildings will monitor external conditions, adjusting their window shades and solar panels depending on whether it's sunny or cloudy.

Sharing energy

With advances in the storage and transfer of energy, future buildings will be able to share their energy. So, during quiet periods, a building will send its excess energy to busier buildings. Buildings will also obtain more of their energy from their immediate environment, using ground source heat pumps and solar panels.

Buildings of the future are likely to be more intelligent, sustainable and flexible than those of today. The 'Internet of Things' – a network of tiny computers that, in the future, will be installed in everyday objects, from toilets to elevators – should enable buildings to meet our needs for energy, ventilation and sanitation more efficiently. Sensors will monitor how many people are in a building and where they are, and will direct heating, lighting and air-conditioning only where it's needed.

Flexible designs

Future buildings will no longer be rigid structures, but will be designed for flexibility, so they can adapt to changing uses. Rooms and even entire floors can be added or taken away, due to their modular construction (made up of a number of independent units).

Robot builders

Robots are already able to lay bricks and paving stones, and aerial drones are being used by surveyors to map sites. In the future, the construction industry is likely to make ever more use of robots and artificial intelligence.

Fascinating fact

The first kilometre-high building is now under construction. The Jeddah Tower in Saudi Arabia, once completed, will be 1,008 metres (3,307 feet) high, with 167 floors.

Printed buildings? Already, crane-like machines can print concrete walls to which doors, windows and roofs are then added. These could be used to quickly rehouse people following natural disasters.

27

Bamboo-reinforced concrete

Traditionally, steel rebar is used to reinforce concrete. But as the cost of steel rises, bamboo might provide a cheap and sustainable alternative. Bamboo fibres can be mixed with an organic resin to create a durable material that doesn't rot. Bamboo absorbs CO_2 from the atmosphere while growing, so it's also good for the environment!

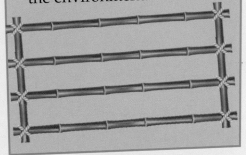

The future of building materials

Future buildings will incorporate new materials that will be lighter, stronger, more flexible and more durable than existing ones, or better at resisting the wind, rain or the dangers of fire. There may even be materials that do completely new things. For example, scientists have developed a self-healing concrete – it's ordinary concrete mixed with bacteria that can seal cracks and fight moss. Or, for those who love a mossy wall, there's now a form of 'bio-receptive concrete' that's designed to promote the growth of moss.

When timber is burned at high temperatures without oxygen (pyrolysis), it produces biochar – a strong, durable, fine-grained form of charcoal. Architects may use biochar as a facade on buildings.

It's okay. I self-heal.

Phone-blocking paint

A new kind of paint has been developed with special properties that obstruct the flow of radiation, blocking mobile phone and television signals. This could be useful in buildings where security and privacy is important, such as government offices and prisons.

Hello? Hello? I can't get any signal!

Musical tiles

Spider silk is five times stronger than steel, and may have potential in the future as a building material – if scientists can work out how to synthesise it in the laboratory. Spider silk has strong resonance properties, so tiles and panels made from this substance could provide very good acoustics in concert halls.

Good sound quality in here!

A new kind of fire-resistant plywood is being made from layers that have been immersed in a liquid fire retardant. Treated in this way, the plywood doesn't burn.

Fascinating fact

Graphene has been called the world's first two-dimensional material, since it consists of sheets of carbon just one atom thick. As well as being super strong and extremely light, graphene also conducts electricity. A graphene-based ink has been developed to print electric circuits directly on a wall. This could make building walls interactive, with data displayed at the touch of a finger.

29

Glossary

Acoustics The qualities of a space that determine how well sound is transmitted in it.

Adobe An ancient building material made from earth. *Adobe* is Spanish for 'mud brick'.

Aggregate Pieces of broken or crushed stone and gravel used to make concrete.

Amphitheatre An open, circular or oval building used to present dramatic or sporting events.

Aqueduct A bridge carrying a waterway over a valley.

Architecture The art and practice of designing buildings.

Basilica A large rectangular hall supported by a double row of columns, used in ancient Rome as a public building.

Cladding A covering or coating on a structure or material.

Concrete A material made of aggregate, sand, cement and water that can be spread or poured into moulds, and hardens to form a stonelike mass.

Contractor A builder or firm that is contracted to construct a building.

Excavator A large machine for digging and moving earth.

Fire retardant A substance or material that does not easily burn.

Flying buttress A structure slanting from a column to form an arch with the wall it supports.

Greenhouse gas Any gas, such as carbon dioxide or methane, that adds to global warming.

Ground source heat pump A heating system for buildings that obtains its heat from below ground.

Grout A paste for filling crevices, such as the gaps between wall tiles.

Hydraulic Describing a mechanical system that works by moving liquid through a confined space under pressure.

Insulator A material used in buildings to prevent heat loss.

Modular construction A form of construction in which a building is made up of separate interlocking sections, or modules.

Pediment The triangular upper section at the front of a Greek temple or other classical building.

Plasterboard Board made of plaster, used to line the inner walls of buildings.

Plinth The projecting base of a building or wall.

Pulley A wheel with a grooved rim around which a cord passes; used to raise heavy weights.

Rammed earth A method of constructing building foundations, floors, and walls by compressing a damp mixture of earth, sand, gravel and clay.

Reinforced concrete Concrete in which metal bars have been embedded to increase its strength.

Sanitation The department of a city or town that handles provision of drinking water and sewage disposal.

Scaffolding A temporary structure outside a building used by workers while constructing or repairing a building.

Smelt Extract metal from its ore by a process of heating and melting.

Stucco Fine plaster used for coating wall surfaces.

Survey (verb) Examine and record the features of an area of land prior to building on it.

Sustainable Describing an object or process that conserves the environment by avoiding the depletion of natural resources.

Treadwheel A large wheel turned by the action of people or animals treading on steps fitted into its inner surface, formerly used to drive machinery.

Vault An arched roof, typically found in churches and other large, formal buildings.

Ventilation The supply of fresh air to a building.

Index

A
adobe 6, 14
arches 6 8, 9
architects 5, 8, 10, 11, 12–13, 14, 18, 20, 21, 22
architectural models 13, 25

B
bricks 6, 8, 9, 11, 14, 16, 21, 27
building sites 16, 17
Burj Khalifa 19

C
CAD 12, 13
cathedrals 8, 9
cement 15
clay 6, 11, 14
Colosseum 7
columns 6, 8, 9, 19, 21, 24
concrete 7, 14, 15, 20, 21, 24, 28
construction 5, 6, 7, 8, 9, 10, 11, 16–17, 18, 19, 22–23, 27

D
deconstruction 22, 23
demolition 5, 10, 22, 24–25
design 5, 10, 11, 12–13, 18, 19, 22
domes 7, 8, 9, 14, 21

E
excavators 24, 25
explosives 24, 25

F
fire resistance 15, 20, 21, 28, 29
floors 12, 13, 16, 17, 24, 25, 27
Florence Cathedral 8
foam 14, 15
foundations 16, 21
framework 16, 18, 19, 20

G
glass 9, 14, 15, 21, 24
Great Pyramid of Giza 7

I
insulation 15, 17, 22

J
Jeddah Tower 27

M
maintenance 10, 11

N
natural disasters 5, 20–21, 27

P
Pantheon 7
pediments 6
plaster 14, 16
plastic 14, 21
plywood 29
property developers 10, 12
pyramids 6, 7

Q
quarrying 8, 11

R
roofs 6, 13, 14, 15, 16, 17, 20, 21, 27

S
Sagrada Família 17
skyscrapers 5, 18–19, 24
steel 11, 14, 16, 18, 20, 24, 28
stone blocks 7, 8, 11, 14
straw 15
surveyors 12, 27
sustainability 5, 12, 14, 22–23, 26, 28

T
Taj Mahal 9
technical drawings 13
timber 11, 14, 18, 20, 28
treadwheel cranes 9

V
vaults 6, 8, 9

W
walls 8, 9, 12, 14, 15, 16, 17, 18, 19, 21, 22, 24, 25, 27, 28, 29
waste 22, 23, 25
windows 9, 15, 17, 19, 20, 21, 22, 24, 26, 27